THE Anxiety Relief Toolkit

THE Anxiety Relief Toolkit

BUILD RESILIENCE WITH PRACTICAL TECHNIQUES AND GUIDED EXERCISES

A GUIDE TO USING YOUR CARDS

Dedication

For all those who struggle. May you find your serenity within these pages.

This edition published in 2025 by Arcturus Publishing Limited
26/27 Bickels Yard, 151–153 Bermondsey Street,
London SE1 3HA

All images courtesy of Shutterstock

AD011270UK

Printed in China

CONTENTS

INTRODUCTION

Courage, Dear Heart.

"Courage is knowing what *not* *to fear."*

Plato

According to the Mental Health Foundation in the UK, who conducted a study in 2022, 59.4% of people surveyed reported that they felt low levels of anxiety on a regular basis, while 40.5% reported that they regularly experienced high levels of anxiety. One wonders what happened to the 0.1% – maybe they were too anxious to respond?

Furthermore, the study also found that women seem to be more anxious than men, experiencing higher levels of anxiety in comparison to their male counterparts. Age can also play a part, with the under 29s suffering more, and the over 70s rarely feeling anxious at all.

Anxiety affects everyone and no-one is completely immune to it. It is an aspect of your basic survival instinct and if you never felt anxious then you probably wouldn't live for very long, because you would be completely reckless! In short, anxiety is one of the things that helps to keep you alive. That said, for some people extreme anxiety can be so debilitating it prevents them from leading a normal life. Feeling anxious every now and then is perfectly natural. Feeling anxious *all the time* is not. It is a sign that your body is out of alignment and that it has become hyper-sensitive.

As a clinical psychotherapist I have witnessed anxiety in all its manifestations, from the subtle tremor of nervousness and apprehension in my clients, to the sheer terror of a full blown panic attack. I have also experienced anxiety myself, so I know how it feels. Anxiety can make you feel stressed, overwhelmed, incompetent, worthless, fearful and highly emotional. It can make you lose confidence in your own ability to cope with life, leaving you timid and afraid, or raging in temper at the wrong people. High anxiety also triggers the release of stress hormones, which in turn can lead to physical health problems later on, but there are things that you can do to overcome it.

In this *Anxiety Relief Toolkit,* I am going to show you how to take back control of your mind and body, so that you can self-regulate, self-nurture and regain your life, using the same techniques I have used successfully with my clients in the therapy room. As we move through these pages you will find information on what anxiety is, how it works, how it builds, where it comes from and why we have it, along with lots of tips and tools to help you to deal with it. In this way you can begin to better understand yourself and where your own anxiety comes from, what your triggers are and more importantly, how to neutralize them so that you can go on to lead a happy, normal life.

I have designed this kit to be as calming and soothing as possible, to nurture you through the stages of anxiety recovery until you are better able to nurture and calm yourself, using the tools I present here. Are you ready to make this journey with me? Then have courage, dear heart, for we are about to take a soft and dreamy approach to a more peaceful life. *You are safe and you are ready for the next step.*

Serene blessings,
Jacqueline Bruce

How to Use the Cards

Along with the book, this kit includes a deck of 50 cards, each with its own message of support and guidance. I recommend that you shuffle and cut the deck at least three times to fully disperse the deck and integrate them properly before you begin to use them. These cards are your psychological tool box. I have split them into five categories, offering positive **Affirmations**, **Self-Soothing** techniques, **Trigger Calming** tips, **Journal Prompts** and acts of **Self-Nurturing**, so that you can access the type of cards that you might need quickly and easily. Each card holds its own subtle power and while these techniques might seem simple on the surface, when used consistently, they can help you to regain your inner peace so that you can create the soft, calm life that you deserve.

There are several ways in which you can use a deck of cards like this one. You can sit quietly and go through them slowly, looking at the words and images on each card, gently absorbing their messages of support. You can cut the deck to reveal a single card each day and focus on that particular message for the duration of that day. You can use a card as a focal point when you meditate, or place it somewhere convenient where you can refer to it throughout the course of the day. Finally, you can shuffle the deck and deal out two or three cards, using their messages in conjunction together to create a calming ritual.

The images on the cards have been chosen carefully so that they are pleasing to look at, with a soft and dreamy focus alongside the optimistic, supportive text. Flipping through this deck is the opposite of doom-scrolling on your phone! They should leave you feeling joyful and optimistic or, at the very least, less fearful. The more you use them, and the psychological tools they suggest, the more powerful they will become, instilling their messages into your subconscious mind, which will in turn create a sense of inner peace and calmness. So without further ado, let us begin our calm and quiet journey into peace and happiness…

CHAPTER 1

The Monster Unknown

Anxiety is a form of fear and could best be described as a deep-seated fear of the unknown. You first experience this emotion during childhood when you might be afraid of the dark, or of the things that might hide in the dark. Anxiety is a child's reaction to the imaginary monster under the bed. Usually people grow out of this type of fear, only feeling it when there is an actual threat, but for a few individuals it can linger, staying with them throughout adulthood.

What Causes Anxiety?

There are many reasons why a fully grown adult might experience extreme anxiety. People who have suffered some kind of trauma also tend to experience a heightened level of anxiety which can last for some time after the traumatic event itself. Mental health issues such as PTSD, ADHD and neuro-divergence can make people more susceptible to anxiety and panic attacks. Hormones can also play a significant role, with development stages such as puberty or menopause often increasing anxiety levels for the duration of these natural transitions. In addition, life changes such as job loss, divorce, illness, injury or bereavement can all increase anxiety and this is perfectly natural.

Anxiety itself isn't the problem. It is the inability to regulate it or to accurately assess whether or not it is a valid response to the situation you are in. Someone who is in a triggered state isn't thinking rationally – they are thinking from a place of panic and survival. If the panic is a logical response to a dangerous situation, such as a city riot, then the anxiety is working as it should, alerting you to potential danger so that you can take steps to remove yourself to a safer place. However, if the anxious panic comes while you are doing something mundane, such as buying milk, then it is a sign that your survival instincts are misaligned and hyper-sensitive. This is more than likely to be due to one of the reasons given earlier, such as past trauma, hormonal changes or overwhelming life events.

Anxiety and Survival

Of course, anxiety isn't *really* about the monster under the bed, nor is it just about how you perceive the unknown. It is simply a mental cog in the workings of the survival instinct and the nervous system. When your brain detects danger, it releases the hormone adrenalin, which leads to feelings of apprehension, anxiety, fear and panic. It can also make you feel nauseated as the body prepares to void any excess weight it hasn't already converted into fuel, leading to vomiting and/or diarrhoea in extreme situations. Again, this is perfectly normal and how your body is designed to work. This adrenalin-fuelled triggering of anxiety is the sign your body needs, in order to go into one of the four main fear responses: fight, flight, freeze or fawn.

Fear Responses

When something scares you, your body is designed to move into its primary fear response. This is unique to the individual and your primary response might not be the same as that of your sister or best friend. Most people gravitate to one main primary fear response, but it is also possible that you might oscillate between two or three, or even all four. This is your instinctive way of trying to find the best way out of a perceived dangerous situation. The main focus of your survival instinct is to keep you alive. When the survival instinct has been triggered, your cognitive functions focus only on survival – everything else turns to white noise. This effectively means that when you are feeling triggered and highly anxious, you are in one of the following fear responses.

Fight – this is quite literally the instinct to fight for your life. You will begin to fight back, *even if the trigger isn't a real threat!* This can lead to antagonistic, argumentative and aggressive behaviour in otherwise peaceful situations. In times of danger, you will tackle the threat head on and try to eliminate it. You may feel that you are constantly having to fight your own corner, which is a sure sign that you might be stuck in the Fight Response.

Flight – as you might suppose, this is the need to run for your life, to put a safe distance between you and the danger. This need to flee can lead you to look for escape routes everywhere you go, to run away from new experiences, people and relationships. Only that which is familiar is trusted. Everything else is perceived as a threat and so the need to flee becomes paramount. You might even make *running* your hobby! Living your life in a constant state of avoidance is a sign that you might be stuck in the Flight Response.

Freeze – this response is interesting because it can often be the most difficult to recognise. It is a much quieter response than Fight or Flight and it has none of their bells and whistles. It presents itself as the need to disappear, to hide, to make yourself small and still, so as not to attract the attention of a predator. This is a very common response in those who have suffered some kind of relational aggression or abuse, where the danger was so close to home their only option was to freeze. Some people live their whole lives in a state of *Functional Freeze*, which is when they create a small, safe life for themselves but rarely venture out of their comfort zone. If you feel the need to lock yourself away in a room for long periods of time, if you only feel safe when you are in solitude, this is an indication that you might be stuck in the Freeze Response.

Fawn – at first sight this doesn't appear to be a fear response at all, just an irritating character flaw, but if we look more deeply it becomes evident that the Fawn Response is a direct correlation to feeling vulnerable. This vulnerability often presents itself as the need to Fawn over anyone who seems bigger, stronger, more powerful or successful than you and can often lead to sycophantic personality traits. People might exhibit this behaviour when they are in ill in hospital or in the care of doctors, because illness is a time of great vulnerability and the doctors hold all the power. A sycophantic, emotionally clingy or people-pleasing nature is an indication that you might be stuck in the Fawn Response.

STEP INTO SERENITY

UNDERSTAND YOUR FEAR RESPONSE PATTERN

Understanding your own personal Fear Response Pattern is the first step towards taking charge of your anxiety because it will give you an indication of when you are in a triggered state, so that you can immediately take steps to talk yourself down from the psychological ledge! It may be that your initial reaction to a trigger, whether real or perceived, is to fight back, followed by a speedy exit and then a period of solitude locked in your house. In this case you would have a primary fear response of Fight, followed by combined secondary responses of Flight and Freeze, with Freeze being the one likely to last the longest. Identifying this pattern is just as important as identifying your personal triggers, because it is your *response* to the trigger that impacts your day to day life the most. We will be looking at ways to break these habitual responses later on, but for now try to identify the Fear Response that you experienced most recently, and work out if it is your primary or secondary fear response habit.

The Negative Effects of Helicopter Parenting

Some people have been brought up in environments that were geared up to create an anxious individual. Obviously an abusive or neglectful childhood can lead to anxiety later in life, but so can the doting parent who wraps their child in cotton wool and constantly hovers over them, ever ready to assist. In psychology we call this *helicopter parenting*, as the parent constantly hovers and circles the child.

There are some parents who simply refuse to step back and allow their children to take risks, have falls and overcome challenges. Instead, they hover around the child, waiting to catch them before they fall, waiting to muffle them in winter clothes at the first fall of a leaf in August, waiting to solve all their problems for them.

This kind of cosseting is extremely harmful and it is a type of *emotional incest*, where the parent cannot let go of the child in a healthy way and remains far too close to them, in an enmeshed and co-dependent relationship. This can last all through life if it isn't addressed. We see a humorous example of this in the 2017 film *Bad Moms Christmas*, where the relationship between Kiki and her mother Sandy, is completely enmeshed and without boundaries. In reality though, it is quite a toxic form of parenting and it can lead to extreme anxiety, low self-esteem and under-confidence in the adult child who, because they were never allowed to fall, never learnt how to pick themselves up. In addition, an overly cosseted child is unlikely to be a high achiever in adulthood because they expect everything to be easy and complain that life is unfair whenever they are expected to work hard for something. They wait for everything they want to just fall into their lap and when it doesn't, they complain about how hard done by they are!

Boundaries are important, even between parent and child. Setting and maintaining strong boundaries is actually an indication of a healthy relationship, so take some time to reassess your relationships and see if any of them are exacerbating your anxiety. If they are then you need to strengthen your boundaries immediately.

Into the Unknown

So far we have looked at where anxiety comes from, how it is attached to your basic survival instinct and how to identify your primary Fear Response. In the next chapter we are going to explore how your own view of the world can either help or hinder the amount of anxiety you experience and what needs to change to bring it back into a healthier state of alignment. Let us go into the unknown and face it together…

CHAPTER 2

Your World View Matters

How you see the world and your place within it has a significant impact on your mental health, including your propensity to anxiety attacks. If you view the world as being a dangerous place, or you think that people are out to get you then you will become very distrustful as a result of that way of thinking. This in turn can lead to increased anxiety whenever you leave the safety of your house. On the other hand, if you perceive the world and the people in it to be inherently good and kind, then you are likely to be less anxious because you expect the best from people.

Your perceptions are largely based upon your previous experiences, so if you have been betrayed or hurt in the past, that experience will colour your perceptions of the world at large. You just need to slightly adjust your associations, because people with high anxiety tend to view life with a certain amount of distrust. They might imagine worse case scenarios or ponder on bad things happening. This is how your imagination can work against you, so if you find yourself thinking along these lines, ask yourself these questions instead:

- *What is the best outcome that could happen right now?*
- *In an ideal world, what would this situation look like?*
- *If the world was full of kindness, how would I expect to be treated?*
- *If the world was full of kindness, how would I treat others?*

- *If the world was a wonderful place, how would I act?*
- *What can I do today to make the world just a little bit brighter for myself and those around me?*
- *If I knew this person had my best interests at heart how would I respond to them?*
- *If I knew that all would be well, what would I do today, tomorrow, next week?*
- *If I knew that I was entirely safe, where would I go?*

Changing your negative associations for positive ones in this way can help to bring your anxiety back down again. Using questions like these can help you to see an alternative reality to the panic-fuelled one you exist in during an episode. This is important, because anxiety and panic often come about when there is no real threat at all – it is simply a *perceived* threat that has triggered your anxious fear response. In psychotherapy we use the following acronym to illustrate this:

F - false
E - evidence
A - appearing
R – real

False evidence appearing real. Think about that for a moment, because that is exactly what extreme anxiety is, in a nutshell. It is when your brain mistakenly identifies something as a threat, based on past experience, and triggers your body to respond accordingly. When was the last time false evidence appeared real to you? What was the external trigger and how did you respond to it?

STEP INTO SERENITY

RE-CONSTRUCTING YOUR WORLD VIEW

One of the easiest things you can do to help minimize anxiety is to re-build your world view. If past trauma has destroyed your optimism, if you know that you have a tendency to be pessimistic or cynical, then that is how the world will appear to you. Changing that perception to something less cynical and more positive is a great initial step towards a softer, calmer and happier life. Take a look at the following examples of how you might choose to see the world, or think up one of your own, and use it as a mantra every day, especially when you're feeling negative or cynical! While they might seem frivolous at first, they are no less powerful for their whimsical nature. Everyone needs a bit of whimsy in their life! It's good for you.

The world is a playground
and I am having so much fun

The world is a dance and I'm having a ball

The world is always kind and benevolent to me

The world might be a circus,
but I am the Ringmaster!

Each day is a fairy-tale and I live my own
happily ever after

Life is but a dream and
all my dreams come true

The world is full of kindness and benevolence,
I see through trusting eyes

My world is enchanting and I live a charmed life

Life is a game and I always win

Types of Anxiety

While there are several ways in which you can experience anxiety, there are five main categories of anxiety disorder. Most people have a low degree of at least one of these disorders, the most common ones being social anxiety and phobias. For instance, think of the number of people who are afraid of heights, or flying or spiders. These phobias are a type of anxiety disorder and they can affect people to varying degrees of intensity. Take a look at the following list and see if you can identify which of these anxiety disorders most resembles your own fears and triggers.

Generalized Anxiety Disorder – this is quite a common branch of anxiety disorder and it presents itself as the constant feeling of worry, fretting, fearfulness and nervousness. It leads to excessive worry about normal everyday things and catastrophic *what if* scenarios playing over in your head. Something as simple as catching the bus becomes a huge task, as you wonder *what if the bus is late or missing, what if it breaks down, what if I get the wrong bus by mistake and finish up lost?* This type of anxiety is applied to most mundane events, meaning that you spend your time worrying about things that are unlikely to happen, rather than enjoying your life. This can also lead to Obsessive Compulsive Disorder, which is when someone creates rituals to try and stave off the perceived disaster. OCD then becomes yet another form of anxiety, along the lines of *Did I lock the door three times before I left the house? I'd better go back and do it again.* And so it continues, day after day after day.

Social Anxiety Disorder – this is another common form of anxiety and lots of people have it to some degree. Basically it is the fear of socialising or of being in social environments or large crowds such as parties, concerts, the theatre etc., and it incorporates the fear of public speaking or *being seen*. Social anxiety can lead to people turning down invitations, preferring to stay home, especially if *Freeze* is their primary fear response. In some cases, the invitation is accepted, but the anxiety presents itself in the form of worrying about what to wear, who will be there, how to get there, how to get home safely and so on and so on. Of course making a plan for transportation is sensible and important – stressing about it, is not! That's social anxiety at play and it can even lead you to call the whole thing off, make an excuse for non-attendance or feign illness.

Separation Anxiety Disorder – believe it or not, this one begins way back when you're a baby or toddler. It develops as a result of an insecure attachment to your mother or main care-giver. If there was ever any possibility that your mum wasn't going to be there to take care of you, maybe because she worked full time, she had an illness or an addiction, she was emotionally withdrawn or she might even have made threats to leave in moments of stress, this can lead to a deep fear of being left behind which continues into adulthood and it can affect all of your subsequent relationships. It presents itself in one of two ways – either deep clinginess, especially if *Fawn* is your primary fear response, or a steadfast independence and voluntary isolation because you don't really trust anyone to be there for you. In this instance it frequently runs in tandem with a primary *Freeze* response.

Phobias – many people have some kind of phobia, whether its fear of water, enclosed spaces, open spaces, creepy crawlies or something else. The degree to which you suffer from a phobia will determine how much anxiety it provokes. Some people can't even look at a picture of a spider without panicking, while for others the panic only begins when they see a real one, so although lots of people might have the exact same phobia, the degree of discomfort is a personal response that varies from one individual to the next. Phobias usually go hand in hand with both the *Fight* response i.e. kill the spider, and the *Flight* response i.e. run for help and let someone else deal with the spider for you. Both can lead you directly into the *Freeze* response once the perceived threat is over as you withdraw and take a little time out to calm down again. Please note: people with phobias *know* that their behaviour is irrational, so pointing that out doesn't help and it can seem very unkind and rather judgmental. Instead, *praise* them if they show even the slightest hint of not having a full-blown meltdown in the face of an eight-legged critter!

Panic Disorder – this disorder is exactly what it says it is – the tendency to fall into a state of abject panic at minimal provocation. Usually there is some kind of significant trigger for this, such as a major life event or a bereavement, which leads to a deep distrust that things will work out well and an overall sense of dread. This in turn leads to panic and the feeling that nothing

is within your control. Again, while it may look like an overreaction to an observer, to the person with the panic disorder their response is entirely valid and proportional to their perceived threat. This disorder tends to run in tandem with a *Flight* or *Freeze* primary fear response. It can also incorporate panic attacks, health anxiety and *thanatophobia* or death phobia. Panic Disorder is probably the most extreme anxiety disorder. It could be that previous anxiety issues haven't been addressed and so the anxiety has escalated into a Panic Disorder. It could also be a learned response if a close family member also suffers with it.

Dealing with Panic Attacks

Some people with extreme anxiety also experience panic attacks, which can be a symptom of any of the above anxiety disorders and is not exclusive to Panic Disorder. When you have a panic attack your heart races, you break out into a cold sweat, you shiver and tremble, you cry uncontrollably in a state of shock. It feels as if the world is crumbling to dust all around you but you're the only one who can see it. The perceived threat is huge and seemingly insurmountable, though you might not even know what that threat is. Panic attacks also come with an unhelpful dose of *Mortality Awareness* – in short, you feel like you're about to die within the next five minutes and no-one can help you. If someone were to ask you what was wrong, you wouldn't be able to tell them, because the fact is *nothing* is wrong, and at the same time *everything* is. It's a very difficult mental and emotional conundrum to navigate. At the time of the attack, all your logical brain functions have slowed right down because you've gone into pure survival mode. This is why you can't simply *think* or coerce your way out of a panic attack. So what do you do when one hits you? Either you sit down somewhere safe and wait it out, allowing the panic to move through you until the feeling passes, or you make a plan.

STEP INTO SERENITY

MAKE A PANIC ATTACK PLAN

If you know that you suffer from panic attacks, then it makes sense to prepare for them as much as you can. Panic attacks can happen anytime, anywhere. This means expecting the unexpected. Panic attacks can occur when you are in the supermarket, driving your car, picking the kids up from school, sitting at your desk at work. There is no rhyme or reason to them. Like flashbacks, they just happen. Chances are that you will come out of such an attack more quickly if someone you trust makes an intervention, even if that intervention is done over the phone. Here is a simple plan that you can start to put in place, just in case.

1. Talk to a compassionate and trusted friend, partner or family member first of all. Tell them you've been having panic attacks. Explain what they are and how they make you feel. Tell them there is no warning or knowing when the next one will happen.
2. Ask this person if they will be your support during these attacks, if you can call them when it happens. Tell them you might not be able to speak properly or explain the situation, and that you're likely to be sobbing, so that they know what to expect. Perhaps set up a keyword you can use to alert them to the fact that you're having an attack – a single word that puts them in the picture immediately.
3. Next arrange what will happen if you need to make such a call. Will they come and get you, or contact someone else

to come to you while they stay on the phone. You probably shouldn't drive right away, even once the attack has passed, so who will be your taxi and how will you get your car home? Who will pick the kids up from school, or ring your workplace? Arrange all of this in advance, so that everyone knows what the plan is. Print it out on paper if needs be.

4. Repeat this process with a trusted boss or colleague so they can assist you and get you somewhere safe and quiet if you have an attack at work.
5. Have a care-plan ready for when you get home again. This might be as simple as wrapping yourself in a warm blanket or hugging a hot water bottle. It might include a soothing cup of herbal tea or a medicinal shot of brandy. Talk it through in advance so that your friend knows what you need and where to find these things.
6. If a panic attack happens, or you feel one coming on, deploy the plan and make that call.
7. Think about setting up some kind of formal counselling so that you can deal with any underlying issues privately. This also shares the care-load so that you're not asking too much from a loved one.

Often, seeing or hearing the voice of a loved one is enough to make the panic attack begin to subside. When you feel this happening, don't immediately go back to your normal routine, but allow yourself time to come round properly. A panic attack is a mental and emotional assault on your nervous system, so rest up and be proud of yourself for making and activating the Plan.

CHAPTER 3

Cycles and Spirals

Life isn't just a series of ups and downs, it is a cycle where the same issues may come around again and again. The past is certainly not dead and buried. You carry it within you every day and it has the power to impact your current life. This is especially true if you have some unresolved issues or past traumatic events that you haven't fully addressed. Overcoming things like abuse and bereavement is usually much easier with some type of professional support in place, so formal counselling is something you could consider. Bear in mind that just because you might have already had counselling for an issue doesn't mean that you don't need it again. If something is still bothering you, then this is a sign that extra counselling might be required.

However, even lesser events such as a ticking off from the boss or being humiliated in school as a child, can all leave a lasting imprint on your psyche. For instance, imagine if a young child wet themselves during the school Nativity play and everyone laughed at them. They might never live it down, being teased about it throughout their school days by their peers. Their parents and siblings might still tease them about it in adulthood. It would be unsurprising therefore, if that person carried into adulthood a fear of being embarrassed or humiliated. They might not even be able to laugh at themselves. If left unchecked, this fear could further develop into Social Anxiety Disorder. The person might have been just five years old at the time of the Nativity play, but the anxiety it instilled can last a lifetime. That is how anxiety disorders tend to develop. Something happens that is painful, humiliating or frightening and this difficult emotion is then carried through life, leading to a hyper-sensitive survival system which is easily triggered into a fear response, collectively referred to as extreme anxiety. So in order to find some relief for your anxiety you need to discover where it came from by doing some deep self-excavation known as Shadow Work.

Shadow Work

The psychologist Carl Jung, believed that everything a person repressed or supressed, such as bad memories, abuse, shame, guilt, fear, inappropriate feelings etc. would coalesce and reform as the Shadow Self, which would then impact their daily lives in a negative way. We still use Jung's teachings today in modern psychotherapy and the Shadow Self has become synonymous with everything that is hidden within the personality and the personal history of the individual. Excavating this Shadow Self is known as Shadow Work and it is basically about coming face to face with your own history, in order to understand yourself better and come to terms with your past. Shadow Work highlights why you do the things you do, where your quirks and habits originated from and what hidden aspects of your past are having a negative impact on your life. It is a great way to discover the root cause of extreme anxiety.

STEP INTO SERENITY

SHADOW WORK EXCAVATION

You can begin this Shadow Work excavation by answering the following questions as fully as you are able to.

1. When did you first notice that you had increased levels of anxiety?
2. Did this coincide with a current event in your life such as a bereavement?
3. Do you think it could be a result of hormonal changes?
4. Have you noticed that the anxiety comes in certain situations or when you are around certain types of people? If so, what and who, and how does this make you feel?
5. Do these situations or people remind you of something from your past? If so what and who, and how did they make you feel at the time?
6. Can you make any connections here between the past and the present? Is the anxiety linked to the past, or to the present situation?
7. Can you identify specific triggers for your anxiety? What do these triggers remind you of?

8. Is the anxiety related to certain types of stress and if so, how can you take steps to minimise this stress?
9. Have you ever had a panic attack and if so do you know what triggered it? Was it one thing or an accumulation of things?
10. Were you ever considered to be an anxious child? If so, what kind of things made you anxious back then: do they still have the same effect or did you grow out of these anxieties?
11. How attached are you to anxiety? Do you believe that you can overcome it with practice?
12. In answering these questions, have you made any links that might help you to know where the anxiety is rooted? If so, what can you do to deal with the root cause?
13. If your anxiety is rooted in your past, how will you address this? With counselling, journaling, a conversation with someone or something else?
14. If your anxiety is rooted in the present, how will you address this? With counselling, journaling, a conversation, making some changes, or something else?
15. Do you believe you have the power to live a calm, happy and peaceful life? If so, how? If not, why not?

Once you have answered this questionnaire you might be able to see certain connections, links, and triggers that you hadn't noticed before, so you can begin to address them by making any changes necessary. This might mean minimizing the time you spend with certain people or taking steps to become more comfortable in certain situations so that they no longer act as a trigger. Stepping out of a fear response becomes easier if you know what it is that you fear and where that fear comes from. Bear in mind, that there is no need for the adult of our earlier example to fear social situations, because he is no longer likely to wet himself in public! His FEAR is *false evidence appearing real* and it is rooted in an episode of his personal history i.e. the Nativity play.

Avoiding the Spiral

Living with an anxiety disorder can feel like you are trapped in a downward spiral, constantly waiting for the next perceived threat to trigger you, bouncing from one fear response straight into the next. It's exhausting, debilitating and generally unpleasant, but it is important to keep in mind that anxiety itself isn't actually harmful. Yes, it's uncomfortable and disturbing, but having a bout of anxiety cannot actually hurt you in any way.

STEP INTO SERENITY

COMING OUT OF A FEAR RESPONSE

As we have already stated, anxiety is really just your body's way of trying to keep you safe. So how do you escape the revolving door of fear responses? Here are some tips to help you.

Step Back – step away from whatever situation you are in. This removes you from the trigger and allows you time to move onto the next step.

Assess the Situation – assess whether or not the trigger was an actual danger and if there is a genuine threat to your life. Chances are there isn't, it's just your survival instinct working overtime. Thank it for doing its job so well, then reassure yourself that there is no danger.

Remember to Breathe – when your body is in a state of high alert your breathing becomes shallow and fast and you might begin to hyperventilate. Regulate this by taking three deep breaths and focus on taking air into your lungs.

Be Aware of Your Self-Talk – keep your internal dialogue positive. Don't berate yourself for feeling anxious or being triggered. Accept that it has happened, and tell yourself that you are handling it in a positive way using the skills you are learning here. See it as an opportunity to put your new skills into practice and give yourself a pat on the back. You're doing great. You're okay. You've already survived worse than this. Everything is going to be just fine.

Recall a Happy Moment – think back to a time when you felt happy and safe. It could be a favourite holiday, a walk in the countryside, riding your horse or your bike, ice skating in winter. Whatever it is, bring it to mind and focus on it for 5-10 minutes.

Listen to Soothing Music or Guided Meditations – listen to something soft and soothing. This will help to create a safe mental space as the music soothes your mind.

Consider Upskilling Yourself – take steps to make yourself stronger. This could mean going to the gym or taking up self-defence classes. It might mean improving your driving skills. Do something that helps you to feel more capable and better able to take care of yourself.

Gentle Exposure Therapy – gradually expose yourself to your triggers and become more comfortable with them (see Chapter 7). Teach yourself that there is nothing to fear from large crowds of people, or barking dogs for example. Have a trusted companion with you when you do this and gradually build up your resilience from just a few minutes' exposure to a few hours. In this way you are re-training your survival instinct that this thing isn't a threat to your life, so there is no need to go into a fear response.

Little Treats for Little Wins – when you have brought yourself out of a fear response, or you have successfully navigated something that once acted as a trigger, give yourself a little treat as a reward. Take a trip to the cinema, have a nice meal, book an afternoon tea, read a new book. Do something that is just for you. This is the equivalent of your teacher giving you a gold star when you did well in class as a child – give yourself the gold star and acknowledge your victories.

Softly, Softly

Now that you have located the possible root causes for your anxiety and know how to escape an unnecessary fear response, it's time to work on creating a life that further supports your recovery journey. In the next chapter we are going to look at how you can move away from harshness and curate a much softer, calmer life for yourself, so read on.

CHAPTER 4

A Soft and Dreamy Approach

The opposite of anxiety is inner peace. Recovery from an anxiety disorder therefore is the active pursuit of inner peace and a state of calm. No-one else is going to do this work for you. It has to come from you, from within, which means that you need to make a mental shift in identity and in how you curate your life. While there will always be external factors that increase your stress levels or trigger a fear response, learning to minimise their effect on you is the key to overcoming anxiety and it begins with how you view yourself.

Are You an Anxious Person?

If you came into my therapy room and I asked you if you are an anxious person, what would you say? If your answer is *yes,* then that needs to change immediately! Answering in the affirmative means that you are *attached* to the anxiety as a personality trait, but it isn't a personality trait. It is a stress response that moves through you from time to time. *Anxiety isn't who you are!* It's just what your body does when your survival instinct has been accidentally activated.

So the first step to making that mental shift we mentioned earlier is to adjust your self-identity, because while ever you keep defining yourself as an anxious person, that is what you are training your mind to be. You cannot step out of anxiety if you see it as being a part of you, any more than you can step away from your own heart! So you need to redefine your relationship to the anxiety disorder. This mental adjustment might be difficult at first, depending on how long you have defined yourself as an anxious person, but eventually it will become easier to detach from the anxiety, accepting that it is a temporary stress response and it doesn't make you who you are.

STEP INTO SERENITY

CREATE A MORE POSITIVE IDENTITY

Replacing the old anxious identity with a new one will take a bit of time, but using the following affirmations can help to speed up the process.

I might experience anxiety from time to time, but I am getting better at overcoming it.

Anxiety is a temporary feeling and I know it will pass.

Anxiety moves through me and I let it go freely.

As uncomfortable as it is, anxiety cannot harm me in any way.

I can always find my inner peace.

My sense of calm and strength of will are stronger than anxiety.

I am safe and I am in charge of my emotions.

I can regulate my own response to stress.

Change Your Mental Landscape

Like identity, your mental landscape also has a part to play in your recovery. The things you fill your mind with can have either a positive, negative or neutral effect on your mood and state of mental health. The saying *garbage in, garbage out* applies here. In order to create a sense of inner peace, you need to fill your mind with peaceful things. This often means avoiding the spools of negativity that come from news programs, newspapers and social media. We often talk about curating our feed when it comes to popular social media platforms, so that they only show us the things that we are interested in. The same thing should apply to your mind. What you feed it matters, so take steps to curate a lovely mental feed of calm, peace and joy.

Try to think of your mind as an Instagram grid. What does it currently look like? Is it filled with images of war, abuse, disaster and catastrophe? Or is it a haven of peaceful images, positive mantras and kind-hearted comments and quotations? Would you *want* to follow an Instagram account that looked exactly like your current mental landscape, or would that be too much like doom scrolling? Your mind is your own personal platform and it is the only one that really matters, because it is the one that feeds directly into your mental health. Keeping it healthy means ensuring that you are curating a peaceful inner landscape by modifying the things you allow your mind to consume. This is entirely within your own control.

STEP INTO SERENITY

CURATING YOUR MENTAL GRID

Take a pen and a piece of paper and make a few notes of what you want your inner mental grid to look like. Is it full of nature and animals, soft pastel shades or bright happy colours, favourite hobbies, books and sports, culture and the arts etc? Now make a list of all the things that *don't* belong on the grid – war, violence, greed, famine, shame, insecurity and so on. This second list is an indication of all the things you need to avoid in terms of mental consumption, so that might mean not watching the news anymore, and unfollowing certain people and accounts on social media. It could mean disabling your social media altogether. Now fill that void by actively consuming all the things on your *first* list instead – nature, animals, soft colourways, happy events and hobbies and so on. In this way you are filling your mind with soft, happy things and so that is what will be fed into your mental health, leading to a gradual decline in things to be anxious about.

It Is Beyond My Control

Often people become anxious about things that are global events such as wars, natural disasters, environmental issues, dictatorships etc. While it is perfectly natural to be upset by these things and it shows a deep level of compassion for humanity, if such external events are making you severely anxious in your daily life then they are having a very negative impact on you.

One of the key factors in anxiety recovery is learning to distinguish between the things that you can and cannot control.

STEP INTO SERENITY

USE SOFT POWER

If one of the root causes of your anxiety disorder lies in global issues, then you need to accept that you are probably not in a position to prevent such events. If they are still upsetting to you, then think about the things you *can* do to help the situation. This might mean donating clothes and toys to a humanitarian aid centre, or raising money for a particular charity. It could mean helping out at a food bank or homeless shelter, or volunteering with an animal rescue charity. This is a form of *soft power.* Your personal soft power is something you *do* have control of and you can decide how and where to use it. While it might not change the world overnight, it can still make

You cannot prevent war from breaking out, or earthquakes and volcanic eruptions from happening. You cannot stop the flood water from rising, or turn back time so that the motorway bridge never collapsed. Internalising these incidents as if they are entirely your responsibility is actually a very subtle form of narcissism, but of course you simply don't have the power to stop such things, so why would you feel responsible for them? *You are not to blame for global or societal issues that you can't control,* so release these responsibilities and let them go, because they are not serving you.

a significant difference, particularly to the people and animals that you are helping.

The act of actually doing something to help others in dire situations not only highlights how privileged you are to be in a position to offer such assistance; it can also lower your anxiety levels because you are being pro-active, giving yourself a sense of purpose and living from a place of compassion for others, which in turn takes you out of your own head for a while. There's no point sitting at home worrying about things you can't change. Either take steps to help in whatever way you can, or accept that it is simply beyond your control. And never underestimate the global impact of soft power. It really can make all the difference.

STEP INTO SERENITY

MAKE A SOFT AND DREAMY VISION BOARD

Surrounding yourself with calming images can act as a visual cue leading to a much calmer mind. We will be looking at creating a calming environment in a later chapter, but for now consider making yourself an anti-anxiety dream board. This is a great way to ensure that you have a collection of soothing images whenever you need to focus on the more calming aspects of life, which can help you to overcome a stressful day or a particularly bad bout of anxiety. You can make the board using physical materials such as poster board and cuttings from magazines, or you can curate one online using a website such as Canva. To begin, collect lots of images that you find especially soft and dreamy. These should be pictures that have a calming and soothing effect on your mind. Once you have your images, arrange them in a pleasing way and glue them to the poster board, or create the board digitally. Place the dream board somewhere you can see it every day, so that it has a soothing effect on you. Some soothing images you might consider adding to the board include:

Swans gliding on lochs and lakes, especially at sunset or in snow.

White doves.

Winter snow scenes and alpine views.

Serene forests and woodlands.

Ocean waves.

Golden beaches and sandy shores.

A sleeping cat or dog.

Your own pet.

Your family in happy times.

Balloons, champagne, cake and scenes of happy celebration.

Symbols of optimism such as hummingbirds, rainbows, and the sun.

Dreamy symbols such as the moon, owls and starry skies.

Your favourite colour and hobbies.

Soft, white feathers.

Dream catchers.

Fairy-tale castles, country cottages, places that signify safety to you.

Angels and angel wings signifying protection and guidance.

Over-thinking Leads to Overwhelm

Over-thinking is when your internal voice goes into overdrive, creating a constant mental chatter that is largely negative and unhelpful. In psychology we refer to this rapid-fire chatter as the *Monkey Mind* because it is constantly flitting from one thing to the next, like a monkey who is easily distracted and easily distressed. We all have a monkey mind and it is not a character flaw, but it can get out of hand if left unchecked.

When the monkey mind is in charge you will have a tendency to over-think *everything*. This in turn, leads to the feeling of being completely overwhelmed. Signs that you are being influenced by your monkey mind include pacing, rapid chatter – both internal and external, inability to concentrate on one thing at a time, constantly being distracted, having very scattered and fragmented thoughts, saying yes to everything out of fear of missing out then realising you've taken on far too much!

When this happens, it is time to go back to basics and focus on your breathing. Making a list in order to prioritise and delegate tasks can also be helpful as it organises your thinking more logically and brings your mind back into alignment, rather than allowing it to fire off in all directions at once. Remember – *just because the monkey invites to the circus doesn't mean that you have to follow all his tricks!* Be calm, be still, be human!

CHAPTER 5

Prioritize Peace

You can't remain calm and collected if you are constantly surrounded by chaos, drama and disorganization. Living a chaotic lifestyle will inevitably lead to some form of anxiety because your nervous system is continually reacting to your external landscape and becoming triggered by it. It is essential therefore, that you take some practical steps to prioritize your peace.

System Overload!

There are various nervous systems in your body, but the two that have a direct impact on anxiety are the *Sympathetic Nervous System* (SNS) and the *Parasympathetic Nervous System* (PSNS). The Sympathetic Nervous System is the one that reacts to your external surroundings and stress, becoming triggered and activating your fear response, be this Fight, Flight, Freeze or Fawn, and as stated earlier, its job is to keep you alive. This is the system that has become oversensitive in people with high anxiety and panic disorders, creating a sense of hypervigilance.

Your Parasympathetic Nervous System on the other hand, is the one that takes charge when you sleep, rest, meditate and relax. Its job is to keep all the other functions and organs of the body ticking over nicely during times of rest and repose. It is this nervous system that slows your breathing when you fall asleep and controls your metabolism, meaning that you can continue to digest food as you sleep. It keeps you in a relaxed state of calm, so when your PSNS is in charge, you feel relaxed, calm, rested and at peace with yourself and the world around you.

One of the main functions of the Parasympathetic Nervous System is to regulate your recovery from stressful situations and your emotional response to them, or your bounce-back ability. In people with anxiety disorders however, this regulation is somewhat slower because the Sympathetic Nervous System refuses to relinquish control, constantly looking for the next threat, so the PSNS doesn't get a look in until you have fallen into a stressed out sleep! Fortunately, you can learn to activate your PSNS yourself, training it like a muscle, though it does take some practice.

STEP INTO SERENITY

ACTIVATE YOUR PARASYMPATHETIC NERVOUS SYSTEM

In Chapter Three we looked at how to step out of a fear response. Now we are going to take that one stage further by activating your Parasympathetic Nervous System, allowing it to take charge and regulate your emotions, by reassuring your Sympathetic Nervous System that there is no threat and it is reacting to a false alarm. You can use these steps immediately after you have stepped out of a fear response, or you can do them as a daily exercise to speed up your recovery from an anxiety disorder.

1. **First use reassuring self-talk to de-activate your SNS.** Say things like: *I'm okay: I'm safe: It was just a false alarm: There is no danger: I'm having a nice time and all is well: It is safe for me to proceed: It is safe for me to relax now, because there was no danger.*

2. **Next deliberately slow down your breathing.** You can use the square breathing method for this, which is where you breathe in through your nose for a count of four, hold it for four, breathe out through your mouth for four, then hold your breath for four and repeat. This will help to regulate your breathing, which in turn activates your PSNS.

3. **Now step outdoors for a few minutes**. Focus on something beautiful, such as a flower or pretty clouds. If you can, go for a walk in nature and enjoy a slower pace of life for a time.

4. **Finally, allow your PSNS to take charge.** Try to act upon its prompts. If you feel sleepy take a nap, if you want to meditate for five minutes find a quiet space (even if this means using the bathroom at work), listen to gentle music or the sounds of nature and bring yourself back into a state of calm. When you feel relaxed and at peace this is a sign that your PSNS is in charge and you have successfully turned down your SNS.

Make Your Systems Work for You

Exercising your PSNS in the above way will help to make sure it functions properly, which in turn will mean it speeds up your recovery from stress and accidental triggers. Strengthening the PSNS also has the effect that it can begin to over-ride the SNS, lowering hypervigilance and making you less likely to be triggered by everyday activities and events. Remember that although both these systems kick in automatically, you are in charge of how you respond emotionally, so if your SNS has activated to a false alarm, simply state to yourself: *Thanks for keeping me safe, but I've assessed the situation and there is no danger, it's just a false alarm.* Then if necessary, move into the exercises for stepping out of a fear response, followed by those that activate your PSNS instead. Repetition of these two exercises will help you to take back control and will speed up your recovery from anxiety.

Self-Monitoring for Peace

It is your responsibility to prioritize your peace. No-one else can do it for you, so you need to know who and what disrupts it in the first place. This can be easier said than done because in the modern world, you are interacting with so much. Thanks to social media and the internet, people now take on board vast amounts of information in a single day – far more than they would have done in a lifetime a few hundred years ago. This obviously has an impact. You also have the ability to connect with more people and world events, even those that are on the other side of the world. The down side to this global village is information overload! You brain simply isn't designed to cope well with it all.

Hopefully by now you will have gone through all your social media accounts and unfollowed those that have a negative impact on your mood and mental health. You might also have stopped watching the news too. Yet it is impossible to switch off completely because the people you know will most likely refer to things they've seen online or on the TV, so you still receive information by proxy.

While switching off from the world completely might be unrealistic, you still need to make your personal inner peace a priority. You can do this by applying the same principle you used with social media to the people in your daily life, and by monitoring your own emotional response to those you interact with regularly. Is there someone at work who is a verbal doom-scroll, always harping on about the state of the world and how hopeless it is? How does your nervous system respond to this person? Does it zone them out and go into its PSNS, or does it raise a false alarm from its SNS, leaving you feeling triggered and equally hopeless? Bear in mind that they might be communicating from their own false alarm and a SNS triggered state, so try not to let them trigger you too!

Protecting Your Bubble of Peace

Just as you worked your way through all your social media accounts and unfollowed those that you found triggering, now you need to do the same for the people you know in real life, creating a social bubble that is peaceful and serene. If someone is having a negative impact on your mental health then it is perfectly acceptable for you to either stop seeing them altogether, or minimize the time you spend with them. If they are someone you work with, then have the briefest interactions with them that you can manage. Just because you work with someone doesn't mean that they are good for you! Not everyone in your life will have your best interests at heart. Some will be serving their own agendas. Make it easier on yourself by not engaging with them and put your personal peace first.

Negative Noticing

Something else that you can do to protect your peace is to be more aware of how you *notice* the world around you. Again, this is a form of self-monitoring and whereas in the last exercise you were noticing your emotional responses to people, in this section you are going to *notice how and what you notice.*

In psychology we often talk about *negative noticing* which is when you focus mostly on all the things you don't like, things

STEP INTO SERENITY

CURATE YOUR SOCIAL BUBBLE

For the next couple of weeks, gently monitor how you feel after interacting with all the people in your current circle. Focus on one individual at a time and ask yourself how you feel when you walk away from that person: lighter, brighter, happier? Down and out and miserable? Or hopeless and fearful? Your emotions are a great highlighter of whether someone is good for your mental health or not. If you feel bad after speaking to someone, do remember that they too could be dealing with their own anxiety issues, so be compassionate, but lessen the amount of time you spend with that person.

As you work through your circle of friends, family and acquaintances you will soon begin to notice who you need to spend less time with. In this way you can begin to curate an inner circle of people who are uplifting and supportive of you and vice versa. This is your social bubble. Protect this bubble and don't let anyone make you feel bad for having a smaller group of friends, or for excluding them from it. If someone accuses you of living in a bubble, in a spiteful way, take it as a compliment because it means that they have noticed that you keep your social group private and peaceful, as you rise above the drama, safe in your bubble of peaceful friends and family.

that didn't go as planned, people that are rude to you and so on. Negative noticing is very bad for your mental health and that of the people around you. There are some people who spend their whole life in a constant state of negative noticing, who fixate on that one thing that went wrong – for instance, the bus was late and over-crowded – and barely notice all the good things that happened that day – they got a free coffee, the weather was nice, the boss praised their work, they won at bingo etc.

Obviously, negative noticing can exacerbate an anxiety disorder and lead you into a triggered state and a fear response, yet it is surprising how many people do it without even realising. Start to notice *how* you notice the world around you and the mundane events of the day. Notice what you tend to focus on the most. What does your mind automatically zoom in on? If you discover that you have a habit of negative noticing, challenge yourself to find three positive things for every negative one. In this way you will break the habit and become a far more positive, and therefore less triggered, person. You might also like to make a practice of actively looking for positive things to notice as you go about your day to day life. Great things are happening in the world every day, but you have to stop and notice them to feel the boost of happiness they have to offer.

CHAPTER 6

Make Space for Joy

Experiencing joy is good for your mind, body and soul. Not only does a feeling of joyfulness lower your blood pressure, it can help to boost your immune system, lower your stress levels and relax your muscles. Mentally, joy can help to increase your sense of optimism and stimulates the release of endorphins, which are the happy hormones. Happy people tend to look on the bright side of any given situation. They are adept at finding the silver lining, even in difficult circumstances. Joyfulness then, is a vital component of recovering from an anxiety disorder, yet when you are in the midst of an anxious meltdown, it can be tough to find anything to be joyful about.

When you were a child, the adults around you will have taken steps to ensure that you had fun things to do and exciting experiences. Whether this was your parents, grandparents, teachers or care givers, it is likely that someone from your childhood will have taken steps to provide you with joyful experiences, to the best of their ability and resources: wonderful Christmases, fantastic holidays, birthday surprises, fun day trips and so on, might all have been a part of your childhood. You probably have at least one happy memory from that time, where something fabulous and unexpected was arranged or given to you. Hopefully you will have lots of happy memories, but unfortunately not everyone has a happy childhood to look back on.

As adults we sometimes forget to prioritize joy. Playtime seems frivolous and something that we should have outgrown, with the more serious tasks of adult life taking priority. We also live in a social culture where busyness is praised and being highly productive is over-valued. We have forgotten how to rest and recharge, how to indulge in frivolous pass-times and playfulness. In short we have forgotten how to create and prioritize our own moments of joy. It could also be argued that organizing your own trips and holidays etc. becomes slightly less joyful when *you* are the one who has to arrange everything, not to mention working hard to pay for it!

Yet it is still important that you incorporate joy into your life, because the benefits are too great to ignore. Doctors tell people who are living with a serious illness such as cancer, to do whatever makes them happy. There is a good reason for this – doctors know that happiness and joy are extremely healing. Step into any hospice and you will see that activities such as art, quizzes and bingo are regular activities that are scheduled into the weekly round. This is because they create a sense of joy and playfulness, which is good for the patients and the families who use those services.

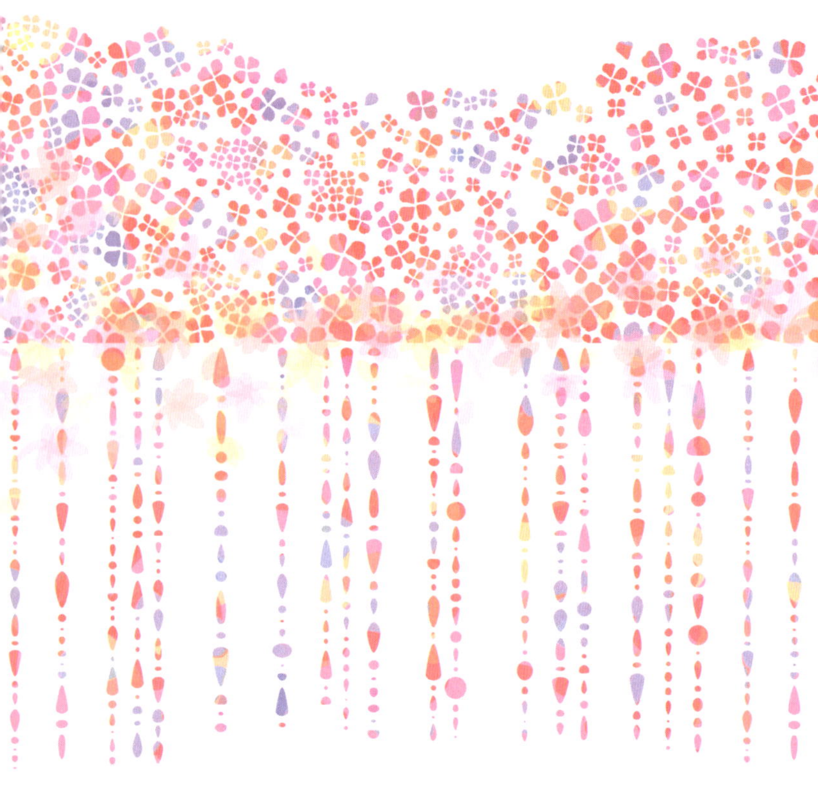

Finding Joy in Anxiety

The effects of joy are the polar opposite of the effects of anxiety on the body. While anxiety raises the stress hormone cortisol, joy decreases it and replaces it with happy, relaxing hormones such as endorphins, dopamine and serotonin. Experiencing joy also activates your Parasympathetic Nervous System, which turns off

the Sympathetic Nervous System and brings about a state of calm. This essentially means that a quick way to over-ride an anxiety attack is to do something joyful, something that makes you happy. Admittedly, when a panic attacks hits you, you are not going to want to start singing and dancing, but you could use a brief moment of joy to shock yourself out of the attack.

STEP INTO SERENITY

WAYS TO INCREASE THE JOY IN YOUR LIFE

Here are a few ideas to help you bring more joy to your life, but bear in mind that what you find joyful is entirely personal.

Laughter is the best medicine - Humour is a powerful tool for anxiety relief. If someone or something makes you laugh, however briefly, the panic will begin to subside. This is because the laughter has triggered the joyful hormones, which will begin to take down the stressful ones within your system. Make sure you have things you can turn to that you know will make you laugh. This could be online videos of funny animals, a DVD or book by your favourite comedian, a funny podcast, a collection of jokes, the phone number of your funniest friend or relative and so on. When it feels like the anxiety is winning, allow yourself to have a funny moment or two and laugh your way out of it.

Understand that the past is gone and it can never be changed – letting go of the past leaves space for more joy to flourish. When you hold on to the past you are in effect blocking the good things from coming into your life. While your past experiences may have been traumatic for you, you survived it and it cannot hurt you anymore. Holding onto it, however, *can* be detrimental to your mental health, so let it go. Release yourself from past regrets, relationships, mistakes and betrayals. Give yourself permission to be free of the past, for the sake of your future.

Be of Service – doing something that serves others is a great way to create more joy. When you help other people, animals or the environment, you are taking steps to increase the joy in your life, because it is impossible to help others without also helping yourself. This is not about virtue signalling. It's about being of service to those who are less fortunate than you are.

Make time for play and fun – schedule some hobbies into your free time and make plans to just have fun! You might take up dancing, ice-skating, tennis or some other activity. If your anxiety is very bad then think of fun things you can do at home, such as painting, writing, handicrafts and so on. Think back to what you enjoyed doing after school when you were a child and make plans to start doing this activity again. Your inner child will thank you for it.

Create meaningful routines – routines are a fact of life, so you might as well make them meaningful and useful to your mental health. See the following section for more tips on this.

The Joy of Routine

We often complain about doing the same things day in and day out and many people think of routine as being rather boring, but in fact it is a great source of safety and comfort. If you were living in a war zone, it would be very difficult to keep to any kind of routine because you would never know when the conflict might affect you and your family. Living with anxiety has a similar effect, in that you never know when an anxiety or panic attack is going to come on. However, your own external world is likely to be a lot more stable than a war zone! It is only your internal world that is in a state of high alert, so creating routines can help to minimize this.

Furthermore, having routines for specific aspects of your life can create more joy and happiness. Think of the cozy comfort of a having a night time routine for the dark winter evenings – you might enjoy a warm bath, soaking in lavender scented bubbles, with a glass of wine or juice beside you, before you put on fresh nightwear and climb into bed with a great book. You could create a routine for after work, by changing into your comfy clothes and making your favourite dinner as you listen to soothing music, before you settle down to watch a film with your partner or family.

Small routines like this not only add structure to your day, they help to make you more mindful of the mundane activities you do all the time. This helps to increase your moments of joy, plus it adds to your overall sense of safety and security. Think of a new routine that you could create and add it into your current schedule. This could be something simple like taking a walk or a drive to the local library every Saturday and borrowing a couple of books to read throughout the week, or it could be walking the dog in the woods and stopping to get a luxury coffee on the way home, or taking flowers to your mum or sister once or twice a month. Routines create a sense of certainty in an uncertain world. They nurture your inner sense of joy, safety and security, which all go some way towards relieving anxiety. How many new routines can you come up with? Pick one joyful or calming routine and begin to implement it over the next week.

Seek Out the Silver Lining

When you're going through a difficult time it can feel as if all the joy and happiness has been sucked out of you and the world around you. This is when you need to work extra hard to seek out the silver lining. There is *always* something to be grateful for if you look hard enough. Silver linings can be elusive – sometimes you really need to dig deep to find one! Rest assured that it is there, waiting to beam its magic into your life, giving you a new reason to smile. In the meantime, remember that you can be your own silver lining - you have a ray of sunshine, a spark of light deep inside you, so let it warm you up and light your way.

CHAPTER 7

Easy Does It

Recovery from an anxiety disorder can take time. It isn't something that happens overnight. Extreme anxiety isn't technically a medical issue – it's a mental health one, because it's your mind and past experiences that trigger your nervous system into a fear response. This can take time to overcome. It takes practice and a lot of self-awareness, which is what you have been working on developing throughout the course of this book. So far we have looked at how to recognize your personal triggers, the signs your body is giving you so that you understand which nervous system has been activated, and which fear response you are in so that you can step back out of it again.

However, you will still have bad days. There will still be times when you feel like this is all a waste of time and that you will never be anything other than extremely anxious, but this is just your fears talking, so try not to pay them too much attention. It is natural to have set-backs and to occasionally feel like you have slipped backwards a little bit on your path to recovery. It is better that you should expect the odd back-slide at the outset of your recovery, than beat yourself up about it when it happens. Three steps forward and two steps back is still a step further on from where you began! You're still make progress, so cut yourself some slack and go easy on yourself. That said, there will always be things that trigger you, so you need to learn how to come to terms with them so that they have a less negative impact on your day to day life.

Gentle Exposure Therapy

In psychotherapy we often use a technique called *Exposure Therapy* which is used to help people who are suffering from extreme phobias and anxiety disorders. It is a way of helping someone to face their fears, by doing so in a safe environment with a therapist that they have come to trust. In this way the client can begin to overcome the fear and desensitize their nervous system to what would once have been a trigger for them.

When you face your fears in exposure therapy you are taking back control and moving towards a more normal way of life. Instead of feeling triggered every time you are in a crowd of people for instance, with exposure therapy you will learn how to regulate your emotional response and get more comfortable when surrounded by people. This can take several months to achieve, but the sooner you begin the sooner you will have neutralized the trigger.

Exposure therapy is something that you can try for yourself, but don't do it alone. Make sure that you are with someone you know well, someone you can trust and who is responsible enough to be able to take charge of the situation should this therapy technique prove to be too much for you at first. Remember that this is about *gradually* exposing yourself to your triggers, not jumping in with both feet! This is also why knowing what your triggers are is important, so that you can begin to neutralize them with a bit of Exposure Therapy. This isn't about berating yourself for being triggered. It is about gently changing your associations.

Types of Exposure Therapy

There are several types of Exposure Therapy, which are designed to gradually build up the levels of exposure until the client has overcome the fear, or at least finds it less triggering and therefore easier to manage.

1. **Imaginal Exposure** – this is the gentlest form of Exposure Therapy and it is when you sit quietly in a safe space and imagine the situation or thing that you find triggering. So if you have social anxiety and you are afraid of large crowds, you would imagine yourself in a room with several people, over time building up the number of people in your imagination. You might begin imagining a small tea-party of five guests and build up to a large arena full of fans at a pop concert or crowds of shoppers at a festive market. The idea is to face the fear in your mind, in the first instance.

2. **Virtual Exposure** – this is another gentle form of Exposure Therapy and it is when you use technology to help you face your fears. If you were afraid of heights for instance, you might watch videos taken from the headcam of a skydiver, rock climber or fast jet pilot. The idea is to face the fear, but from a safe distance, until you are comfortable with experiencing heights or whatever, in a virtual sense.

3. **In Vivo Exposure** – *In Vivo* means *'in life'* or *'in the body'* and this is a significant step forward in Exposure Therapy because it takes place in real life. At this stage, you begin to expose yourself to your triggers and face them in reality, so if you were scared of water you might paddle your feet in the sea or get into the shallow end of a swimming pool. During *in vivo* exposure the sights, sounds and scents associated with the trauma or anxiety can all come into play, as clients are gradually exposed to them again in a safe way. This is a significant leap forward in an individual's anxiety treatment and it means that the client is well on the way to making a good recovery or to being able to manage their symptoms and their personal fear responses in situ.

4. **Prolonged Exposure** – this is the final stage, where *in vivo* exposure is experienced for a prolonged time, gradually building up tolerance, without being triggered. For example, a soldier with PTSD who is triggered by loud noises and explosions might attend a fireworks display for a specific length of time.

I can be changed by what happens to me. But I refuse to be reduced by it.

Maya Angelou

STEP INTO SERENITY

PRACTICE EXPOSURE THERAPY

You can use these Exposure Therapy techniques in your own life to help you overcome an anxiety disorder. Start at the first stage, Imaginal Exposure, and gradually work your way through the stages of Exposure Therapy. Make sure that you are with someone you can trust. Don't use these techniques when you are alone, or at least have a trusted friend you can call on the phone if you need to. Gradually exposing yourself to your personal triggers in this way, is the key to long lasting anxiety relief and recovery. It will help you to desensitize those triggers so that they no longer have a negative effect on you, which in turn means that you can lead a more normal life without the threat of an anxiety attack dogging at your heels.

Exposure Therapy can include re-visiting a place or mode of transport, exposing yourself to the smells, sights and sounds that you associate with the trigger or trauma, listening to a particular song or piece of music until it is no longer triggering, wearing an item of clothing that you associate with past trauma or letting it go by throwing it away, and so on. You can also create a *Fear Ladder* to give yourself a plan to work with.

Practice Self-Compassion

The techniques in this chapter involve some deep psychological work on your part. It can seem very daunting to move through these techniques and you might not be ready to face all of your fears just yet. That's okay. You don't need to do this all at once! In fact, you will get much better results if you take your time. There is no telling how long it will take for you to overcome a particular fear, but so long as you are working on it a little each day, you will make steady progress. Bear in mind that you will have carried some of these triggers and fears with you for a very long time, possibly even since childhood, so you are not going to overcome them in one self-therapy session.

It can be tempting when doing this deep work to isolate yourself and hide away under the duvet, but please don't. You need to have fun as you go, so remember to prioritize your peace and make space for joy, even as you move through this deeper level of Shadow Work. Be compassionate with yourself, practice self-care and let your loved ones know that you are undertaking this deeply personal journey so that they can support you. You have come a very long way already. Be proud of yourself!

STEP INTO SERENITY

CREATE A LADDER OF FEAR

The image of a ladder is frequently used in therapy and while it usually denotes accomplishment and achievement, it can also be used to create a hierarchy of your personal triggers – in this sense it is known as the *Fear Ladder*. This technique is something that you can do easily at home. Take a sheet of paper and draw a ladder that fills the page. Now beginning at the bottom of the ladder, write in your personal triggers and fears in accordance with how panic-inducing they are – so you would write the least panic-inducing fear at the bottom of the ladder and work up to the one that scares you the most, writing it on the top rung of the ladder.

Now you can clearly see how much you are dealing with in terms of fear and how those fears relate to your anxiety and panic disorder. Remember to include things like scents, sounds, tastes, clothes etc. – anything that you associate with trauma or anxiety needs to find its place upon the Fear Ladder. You might need to daft this out a few times to create a ladder that is an accurate reflection of your fears and triggers, as you figure out where they belong in the hierarchy.

These are the things that you can use Exposure Therapy techniques to address, beginning with the fears at the bottom of the ladder and working your way up to the top of the ladder. Remember to take each fear through all four stages of Exposure Therapy before you move on to the next one. Work your way through your triggers and fears in a gradual way, starting with the one that causes the least amount of anxiety and taking it through the stages of Exposure Therapy until it no longer has a negative impact on you, then move on to the next trigger or fear and repeat the process. It may take some time to climb the Fear Ladder, but you can cross each rung off as you overcome that trigger, to show your progress.

CHAPTER 8

Create a Nurturing Environment

Your environment plays a huge role in whether or not you are anxious. From your workplace to your home, you should take steps to try and create environments that are nurturing and calming. While there are limits to what you might be able to do at work, you can still create your own sense of peace in your immediate work area, such as in your car or work vehicle, on your desk and around your computer etc., by having small family photos, crystals, fancy stationery and so on, around you as you work. If you are on your feet all day, moving from place to place, then you can carry small items in your pockets, such as a worry stone, a lavender pulse roller, a small photo of a loved one, which can help to give you a sense of peace as you work. In this chapter we will look at ways that your environment can work against you, so that you can begin to address it.

Clutter, Hoarding and Trauma

Believe it or not, excessive clutter and hoarding is actually a response to trauma. Being surrounded with clutter, piles of rubbish and bits of old junk will undoubtedly add to your anxiety, so if you are currently surrounded by excessive untidiness at home this is something that you need to address as a part of your recovery from anxiety.

Why do we surround ourselves with material possessions? Well, on one hand it helps to personalise your space and make it your own. On the other hand, it can quickly get out of control if you have too much of everything! Your home should be a calm, peaceful retreat, somewhere that you feel safe and supported, but if you have to clamber over piles to stuff whenever you need to go to the bathroom then your environment is actually working against you. Of course, we all have items that mean a lot to us, as well as things that we are not so fond of. The trick to a peaceful and nurturing environment is to make the most of the first category, while eliminating the second. But where does all this clutter come from and how is it linked to trauma and anxiety?

How Clutter Masks Trauma

In psychology we often talk about masking behaviours – that is, habits that help to conceal the hidden trauma that lies beneath the surface. Masking behaviours help people to avoid their own issues for as long as possible, perhaps indefinitely. Hoarding and clutter is a type of masking behaviour and studies have shown that it can actually exacerbate feelings of anxiety, depression, overwhelm and despair. If holding onto clutter is so damaging, then why do some people continue to do it? It is because the clutter represents something important to them, something that they are afraid to let go of.

The Hoarding Instinct

Trauma can trigger the hoarding instinct in some people, which is when they develop a strong emotional attachment to material things. This instinct can even be applied to items of junk and rubbish, such as empty boxes, as the hoarder believes that they might need it at some stage in the future and so they refuse to let it go. Hoarding is disorganised, unhygienic chaos. It is slightly different from collecting because collections are usually curated and kept in good order. However, collections can get out of hand and lead to hoarding too. With hoarding, the individual only feels safe when they are surrounded by things, even if those items are useless or what most of us would consider rubbish and items of waste.

What is interesting about hoarding is that it can cause anxiety in two ways. First the clutter itself creates anxiety, embarrassment and shame. Then the idea of parting with anything creates even greater anxiety and so the hoarder remains stuck. This hoarding instinct is usually triggered by some kind of mental health issue or a traumatic event.

Types of Hoarding and Clutter

Hoarding isn't just a case of having too many possessions, though this is usually how it begins. It often comes from a deep fear of letting go and from fear of change. It can also be a form of self-protection, as people quite literally barricade themselves in behind a mountain of stuff. If it is not addressed, this fear can become severely misaligned, so that even throwing away items of rubbish becomes difficult. If someone is surrounded by empty boxes, dirty food wrappers, old magazines and newspapers etc, then not only is this unhealthy and unhygienic, it is a visible sign that they are struggling with a hidden trauma. There are several types of hoarding, each one relating to a different aspect of trauma and they can all exacerbate an anxiety disorder.

Bereavement hoarding – this is usually an accumulation of items someone has acquired following the death of a loved one. It can include large items of furniture, clothing, jewellery, personal possessions and the collections of the deceased. Understandably, people find this kind of clutter extremely difficult to let go of, as it feels like a betrayal of the deceased, but it is essential to let items go if they are to move through the bereavement process and come out on the other side. Hoarding this stuff only prolongs the grief and keeps people stuck. Keep one or two items for sentimental reasons and get rid of the rest.

Doomsday Hoarding – this is when someone acquires a collection of survival items *just in case* the worst happens. Collections that include crates of bottled water, toilet rolls and sanitary items, medication, canned food, camping equipment, blankets, candles, lighters and matches, batteries and torches and so on, all come under doomsday hoarding, which goes well beyond the

standard power-cut kit most people might keep under the sink! This type of hoarding comes from someone who simply does not trust that all will be well. They are expecting a great catastrophe and they want to be prepared for it, even going so far as to collect empty boxes just in case they need to move home quickly. Often this happens with people who have already been through a catastrophe of some kind. Maybe they have been evicted and suddenly made homeless, or caught up in a conflict or war, or their parents or grandparents were at some point in the past and there is some generational trauma at work. Refugees, asylum seekers, the homeless, evacuees, and their decedents might exhibit this kind of masking behaviour. Keep enough items to see you through a couple of weeks and get rid of the rest. Trust that all will be well.

Comfort Hoarding – this can be a tricky one to identify because comfort hoarding is something most people do to a certain extent. However, when done to excess, it is classified as *Comfort Hoarding or Nesting Hoarding.* As the name suggests, it is when someone gathers together collections of items that make them feel more comfortable, secure, enriched or that signify to them that they now have a very comfortable life. This could be home comforts such as cushions, throws and dinnerware, or personal items like perfume, cosmetics, toiletries and so on. Usually this hoarding occurs in people who have experienced severe poverty in the past when the basics became luxury items because they couldn't afford them. When their financial circumstances improve, they begin to collect all the items they once felt deprived of, ensuring that they have plenty of them. At its root, this stems from a fear that they will once again be thrown back into poverty, so they create a safety net of lovely things. They do this to make any potential future poverty more bearable, by ensuring that they have an excess amount of items that might become unaffordable again. It is about banking everyday luxury that they can then draw upon during times of hardship and poverty. Go through your belongings and donate items that you will probably never use. Imagine them going to someone who is struggling financially and who really needs them, if this makes it easier to let things go. You really don't need three dozen shower gels, so be bold and get rid of some!

Collector's Hoarding – simply put, this is when a beloved collection gets out of control. It might be dolls, figurines, books, shoes, or something else, but if you are struggling to find space for your collection, then it's time to curate it. Go through and weed out anything that you can donate or sell on. Keep in mind the space you have available, the condition of each item (shabby ones will diminish the effects of the collection overall) and the general condition of the collection as a whole. Is it past its best? Does it still give you joy or are you bored with it? Do you know a fellow collector who would love some of your things? Winnow it down, then arrange the remaining items nicely. Consider each purchase very carefully before you add to your collection.

Animal Hoarding – this is perhaps the most heart-rending type of hoarding, but it is actually more common than you might think. Some people collect a menagerie of animals, often believing that they are *rescuing* them, but then neglecting to care for them properly because they have so many. They might collect a random variety of creatures, or stick to a single species – sadly, due to their roaming nature, cats are especially prone to being enticed and then hoarded. Often this kind of hoarding comes about due to loneliness or serious mental health issues in the hoarder. The animals may take over entire rooms or parts of a property, while the hoarder struggles to keep on top of dirty litter boxes and providing adequate food and veterinary care for all the animals. This presents a health hazard to both human and animals. It should be stated here that in many countries animal hoarding is illegal.

If you want to
improve your life,
clean out a closet.

Cheryl Richardson

STEP INTO SERENITY

DECLUTTERING FOR ANXIETY RELIEF

While clutter can have an adverse effect on your stress levels, leading to feelings of overwhelm and to not being able to clean properly because there is too much stuff to clean, decluttering can have a very positive effect on your mental health. Decluttering, cleaning and organising your belongings and your home can make you feel more in control and it makes the home easier to keep clean and tidy.

If you have been struggling with clutter, then take this chapter as a note of reassurance and see if you can identify the kind of clutter you have and where it comes from emotionally. Then begin to declutter, one drawer, one room at a time. Don't do too much as that would be overwhelming. Just do a drawer or a cupboard a day. Save bigger jobs for the weekend, or when you have someone to come and help you. Clutter doesn't make you a bad person. It is simply a life-response to inner emotional trauma and you can get on top of it.

Think of the kind of environment you want to live in and begin to move your home in that direction, one area at a time. Sift, sort, donate and discard accordingly, until you have the kind of space that you find calming, peaceful and nurturing. Once you know the reason behind the clutter it becomes much easier to detach from it and get it sorted. Plus, decluttering helps to regulate the nervous system too, so it's a win-win situation. You might also benefit from having some formal counselling to address the underlying issues that led to the hoarding instinct being triggered in the first place. In the meantime, remember that life is in a constant state of flow – it is safe to let things come and to let other things go. Live in the spirit of *flow* and you are less likely to feel deprived or overwhelmed.

CHAPTER 9

A Second Blooming

Coming out of an anxious period of your life is like a second blossoming. Just as when a panic attack passes you find yourself wondering 'what was that all about?', you may experience a similar feeling once you realize that the anxiety has subsided and it no longer impacts your daily life. Eventually you may have entire days, weeks and months without suffering from anxiety or having a panic attack. This means that your Sympathetic Nervous System has been successfully re-regulated and it is now working as it should, to alert you to actual danger, rather than going off at various false alarms every five minutes. How will you know that you are on the road to recovery and coming out of an anxious disposition? There are many signs to look out for.

Signs of Recovery from Anxiety

At first it might not seem as if much has changed. In fact, you might be navigating events and activities that once made you terribly anxious without actually noticing that you are not reacting to them anymore. Then it will suddenly occur to you how well you are coping! When this happens give yourself a pat on the back and celebrate it as a win and a significant achievement. Try not to worry about *why* you're not anxious! Just accept it, and the fact that you are now having a normal response to your daily round because you have successfully deactivated your usual triggers. This is the result of the effort you have put into your recovery, the deep psychological Shadow Work you've done and the excavation of your past. Other signs of your continued recovery include:

- **Relaxation** - you feel much more relaxed, rather than on high alert all the time. You are no longer hyper-vigilant.

- **Better sleep** – your sleep patterns return to normal and you generally sleep more deeply and wake up feeling refreshed.

- **Better concentration** – you are able to concentrate more easily and for longer periods of time now that the brain fog has cleared and the monkey-mind is a lot less chatty!

- **Emotional Intelligence** – you know when you are about to over-react and you have the ability to calm yourself. Your emotions are appropriate to the situation. No more panic attacks over which type of milk to buy!

- **More Control** – you feel generally more in control of your life and yourself. You have better coping skills and you feel more capable and better equipped to deal with whatever life throws at you.

- **Self-Awareness** – you have greater self-awareness and you are more aware of your thoughts, self-talk, where they come from and how to keep them in check.

- **Joyfulness** – you experience joy on a daily basis, even if it's only at the little things in life. Happiness is no longer a struggle for you, it comes naturally.

- **Peace** – you have made peace with you past and you look forward to the future with brighter optimism, rather than dread and fear. You are busy making plans for new adventures and achievements.

STEP INTO SERENITY

TRY, TRY, AND TRY AGAIN!

If you read this book once and then put it on the shelf, guess what? It isn't going to work! You need to actually *use* the book and the cards as the psychological tools that they are in order to find relief from anxiety. This goes beyond just reading the book, it means *practicing* the psychotherapy techniques that I have presented here, diving into your past even though it can be difficult, and learning how *your* body works so that you can take steps to over-ride its triggers and the fear response (Fight, Flight, Freeze, Fawn) those triggers create.

This is a work book, so feel free to highlight the techniques that worked well for you, or the passages that you found the most comforting and reassuring. Go back to the beginning and re-read it whenever you feel a negative spiral coming on, or when your anxiety is getting out of hand again. Use the book over and over, as many times as you need to and just keep trying! Anxiety isn't fixed overnight, because it didn't build up overnight. It took time to develop and take hold, so it will take time to dismantle it too. Give yourself the time it takes to heal, to recover and to feel that relief.

How Long Will It Take?

Recovery is unique to the individual. It depends on how long you have had an anxiety disorder, how attached to it you have become and the depth of the trauma or stress that triggered it in the first place. If it is your job that made you anxious and you move to a new workplace, the anxiety might stop with the change in work space. If your anxiety comes from a previous trauma it might take longer. It could also be the case that the anxiety disappears, only to return again later during a stressful time. If that's the case then you will need to begin the process again, of identifying your *new* triggers and fear responses and then working to re-regulate the Sympathetic Nervous System once again. Some people are just more prone to anxiety than others, but that doesn't mean that you can't recover from it, because you can. It just takes time.

Go Easy On Yourself

Anxiety doesn't make you a bad person. It is a sign that you have been coping with significant amounts of stress/trauma for a prolonged period of time, or that you are experiencing hormonal shifts and changes. Be gentle with yourself. Treat yourself kindly. Nurture yourself. Being hard on yourself will only make matters worse, so give yourself the reassurance you need. Look for kindness and you will find it. Arrange some formal counselling if you think you need to. Remember that setbacks are normal and they are not a sign of failure. Tomorrow *is* a better day!

CONCLUSION

All Shall Be Well

"All shall be well, and all shall be well,
and all manner of things shall be well."
Lady Julian of Norwich, circa 1373.

Here, as we come to the end of this book, you can rest assured that your journey doesn't end with the closing of these pages. You have come a long way, but now the real journey begins as you put what you have learnt into practice in your own life. You have gathered intelligence, excavated your past, and faced your fears. You have learnt new skills, curated your social circle and created nurturing environments in which to thrive, rather than merely survive. You have learnt that it is okay to prioritize your peace and sense of joy.

I hope that you have enjoyed this soft and gentle approach to overcoming anxiety. Remember that anxiety is a mental health issue, so a logical place to look to for answers is your own mind – your thoughts, your self-talk, your daily habits, your past experiences and so on. By making small adjustments here and there, you can achieve significant positive change in your ability to successfully navigate life and regulate your emotions. You now know how to get your nervous system on board for the journey too, so all that's left for me to say is, good luck and well done! You should be proud of the work that have done and will continue to do, here in the pages of this book. Keep it close by and use the cards daily for the best results. Most of all, bear in mind that today can be a great day, tomorrow is a better day and that all shall be well in the future.

Serene blessings,
Jacqueline Bruce

INDEX

V

W

By the Same Author

Me and Mine Journal (2025). Arcturus.

Further Reading and Resources

BAN BREATHNACH, Sarah (1998). *Something More: Excavating Your Authentic Self*. Warner Books.

CORI, Jamie Lee, (2008). *Healing from Trauma*. Da Capo Press.

HAINES, Steve (2016). *Trauma is Really Strange* (graphic novel). Singing Dragon.

MCLEOD, John (1993). *An Introduction to Counselling*. Open University Press.

MILNE, Aileen (1999). *Understanding Counselling*. Hodder Headline

NEFF, Kristen, (2011). *Self- Compassion*. Harper Collins.

SANDERS, Pete (2011). *First Steps in Counselling*. PCCS Books

STEWART, Ian (2014). *Transactional Analysis Counselling in Action*. SAGE Publications.

WALKER, Pete (2013). *COMPLEX PTSD: From Surviving to Thriving*. Pete Walker Publishing.

WILLIAMS, Mary Beth (2011). *The PTSD Workbook*. Raincoast Books.

Useful Websites

www.singingdragon.com

www.mind.org.uk

www.anxietyuk.org.uk

www.nhs.uk

www.nami.org

www.activeminds.org

Acknowledgments

With special thanks to everyone who played a role in my own journey to becoming a Therapeutic Counsellor, namely my tutors and clinical supervisors: Martin Loughna, Millie Anderson, Carolyn Herwig, Lee Adams and Mary Watton. It was a long journey, but worth it in the end. Thank you, also, to the team at Arcturus for continuing to support my work as a writer and psychotherapist.